PLANNING, PROGRAMMING, BUDGETING, AND EXECUTION
IN COMPARATIVE ORGANIZATIONS

VOLUME 4

Executive Summary

MEGAN McKERNAN | STEPHANIE YOUNG | TIMOTHY R. HEATH | DARA MASSICOT
ANDREW DOWSE | DEVON HILL | JAMES BLACK | RYAN CONSAUL
MICHAEL SIMPSON | SARAH W. DENTON | ANTHONY VASSALO | IVANA KE
MARK STALCZYNSKI | BENJAMIN J. SACKS | AUSTIN WYATT | JADE YEUNG
NICOLAS JOUAN | YULIYA SHOKH | WILLIAM SHELTON | RAPHAEL S. COHEN
JOHN P. GODGES | HEIDI PETERS | LAUREN SKRABALA

Prepared for the Commission on Planning, Programming, Budgeting, and Execution Reform
Approved for public release; distribution is unlimited

For more information on this publication, visit **www.rand.org/t/RRA2195-4**.

About RAND

The RAND Corporation is a research organization that develops solutions to public policy challenges to help make communities throughout the world safer and more secure, healthier and more prosperous. RAND is nonprofit, nonpartisan, and committed to the public interest. To learn more about RAND, visit www.rand.org.

Research Integrity

Our mission to help improve policy and decisionmaking through research and analysis is enabled through our core values of quality and objectivity and our unwavering commitment to the highest level of integrity and ethical behavior. To help ensure our research and analysis are rigorous, objective, and nonpartisan, we subject our research publications to a robust and exacting quality-assurance process; avoid both the appearance and reality of financial and other conflicts of interest through staff training, project screening, and a policy of mandatory disclosure; and pursue transparency in our research engagements through our commitment to the open publication of our research findings and recommendations, disclosure of the source of funding of published research, and policies to ensure intellectual independence. For more information, visit www.rand.org/about/principles.

RAND's publications do not necessarily reflect the opinions of its research clients and sponsors.

Published by the RAND Corporation, Santa Monica, Calif.
© 2024 RAND Corporation
RAND® is a registered trademark.

Library of Congress Cataloging-in-Publication Data is available for this publication.

ISBN: 978-1-9774-1245-4

Cover design by Peter Soriano; adimas/Adobe Stock images.

About This Report

The U.S. Department of Defense's (DoD's) Planning, Programming, Budgeting, and Execution (PPBE) process is a key enabler for DoD to fulfill its mission. But in light of a dynamic threat environment, increasingly capable adversaries, and rapid technological changes, there has been increasing concern that DoD's resource planning processes are too slow and inflexible to meet warfighter needs.[1] As a result, Congress mandated the formation of a legislative commission in Section 1004 of the National Defense Authorization Act for Fiscal Year 2022 to (1) examine the effectiveness of the PPBE process and adjacent DoD practices, particularly with respect to defense modernization; (2) consider potential alternatives to these processes and practices to maximize DoD's ability to respond in a timely manner to current and future threats; and (3) make legislative and policy recommendations to improve such processes and practices for the purposes of fielding the operational capabilities necessary to outpace near-peer competitors, providing data and analytical insight, and supporting an integrated budget that is aligned with strategic defense objectives.[2]

The Commission on PPBE Reform asked the National Defense Research Institute to provide an independent analysis of PPBE-like functions in selected countries and selected non-DoD federal agencies. The commission will use insights from these analyses to derive potential lessons and convey recommendations to Congress on PPBE reform.

This executive summary distills key insights from a series of case studies of budgeting processes across nine comparative organizations, as detailed in the following three companion volumes:

- *Planning, Programming, Budgeting, and Execution in Comparative Organizations:* Vol. 1, *Case Studies of China and Russia*
- *Planning, Programming, Budgeting, and Execution in Comparative Organizations:* Vol. 2, *Case Studies of Selected Allied and Partner Nations*
- *Planning, Programming, Budgeting, and Execution in Comparative Organizations:* Vol. 3, *Case Studies of Selected Non-DoD Federal Agencies.*[3]

---

[1] See, for example, Section 809 Panel, *Report of the Advisory Panel on Streamlining and Codifying Acquisition Regulations*, Vol. 2 of 3, June 2018, pp. 12–13; Brendan W. McGarry, *DOD Planning, Programming, Budgeting, and Execution: Overview and Selected Issues for Congress*, Congressional Research Service, July 11, 2022, p. 1; and William Greenwalt and Dan Patt, *Competing in Time: Ensuring Capability Advantage and Mission Success Through Adaptable Resource Allocation*, Hudson Institute, February 2021, pp. 9–10.

[2] Public Law 117-81, National Defense Authorization Act for Fiscal Year 2022, December 27, 2021.

[3] Megan McKernan, Stephanie Young, Timothy R. Heath, Dara Massicot, Mark Stalczynski, Ivana Ke, Raphael S. Cohen, John P. Godges, Heidi Peters, and Lauren Skrabala, *Planning, Programming, Budgeting, and Execution in Comparative Organizations: Vol. 1, Case Studies of China and Russia*, RAND Corporation, RR-A2195-1, 2024; Megan McKernan, Stephanie Young, Andrew Dowse, James Black, Devon Hill, Benjamin J. Sacks, Austin Wyatt, Nicolas Jouan, Yuliya Shokh, Jade Yeung, Raphael S. Cohen, John P. Godges,

These reports should be of particular interest to stakeholders in DoD's PPBE processes and U.S. government officials who are involved in improving these processes.

The research reported here was completed in March 2023 and underwent security review with the sponsor and the Defense Office of Prepublication and Security Review before public release.

RAND National Security Research Division

This research was sponsored by the Commission on PPBE Reform and conducted within the Acquisition and Technology Policy Program of the RAND National Security Research Division (NSRD), which operates the National Defense Research Institute (NDRI), a federally funded research and development center sponsored by the Office of the Secretary of Defense, the Joint Staff, the Unified Combatant Commands, the Navy, the Marine Corps, the defense agencies, and the defense intelligence enterprise.

For more information on the RAND Acquisition and Technology Policy Program, see www.rand.org/nsrd/atp or contact the director (contact information is provided on the webpage).

Acknowledgments

The authors thank the members of the Commission on PPBE Reform—Robert Hale, Ellen Lord, Jonathan Burks, Susan Davis, Lisa Disbrow, Eric Fanning, Peter Levine, Jamie Morin, David Norquist, Diem Salmon, Jennifer Santos, Arun Seraphin, Raj Shah, and John Whitley—and staff for their dedication and deep expertise in shaping this work. We extend special gratitude to the commission chair, the Honorable Robert Hale; the vice chair, the Honorable Ellen Lord; executive director Lara Sayer; and director of research Elizabeth Bieri for their guidance and support throughout this analysis.

Dedication

These volumes are dedicated to Irv Blickstein, whose decades of experience within the U.S. Navy's Planning, Programming, Budgeting, and Execution community deeply informed this work and whose intellectual leadership as a RAND colleague for more than 20 years greatly enhanced the quality of our independent analysis for DoD's most-pressing acquisition challenges. Irv's kindness, motivation, and ever-present mentoring will be sorely missed.

Heidi Peters, and Lauren Skrabala, *Planning, Programming, Budgeting, and Execution in Comparative Organizations:* Vol. 2, *Case Studies of Selected Allied and Partner Nations*, RAND Corporation, RR-A2195-2, 2024; Megan McKernan, Stephanie Young, Ryan Consaul, Michael Simpson, Sarah W. Denton, Anthony Vassalo, William Shelton, Devon Hill, Raphael S. Cohen, John P. Godges, Heidi Peters, and Lauren Skrabala, *Planning, Programming, Budgeting, and Execution in Comparative Organizations:* Vol. 3, *Case Studies of Selected Non-DoD Federal Agencies*, RAND Corporation, RR-A2195-3, 2024.

Summary

The Commission on Planning, Programming, Budgeting, and Execution (PPBE) Reform asked the RAND Corporation to conduct case studies of the budgeting processes of nine organizations: five international defense organizations (including two near-peer competitors) and four other U.S. federal government agencies. The commission will use insights from these analyses to derive potential lessons for U.S. Department of Defense (DoD) PPBE reform and convey recommendations to Congress.

Overarching Observations

A synthesis of key insights from the nine case studies—and the applicability of those insights to DoD's PPBE System—led to the following overarching observations for the commission:

- There is a need for balance between enabling innovation and agility in military acquisition and ensuring the budget stability and predictability required for complex, long-term development efforts.
- Beyond resource planning processes, military modernization requires a strong and broad-based societal foundation—with a trained workforce, an industrial capacity, innovation policies, national investments, and long-term planning and coordination of these inputs.
- DoD resource planning policies and decisions have implications for defense industrial base health and interdependent, co-development efforts with allies and partners.
- Continuing resolutions and other sources of budgetary uncertainty that impede DoD resource planning are challenges that are not encountered by the allies and partners examined in these case studies.
- Other U.S. government agencies have developed tailored approaches and mechanisms that enable budget flexibility and agility to meet mission needs.
- Resource management processes across the board tend to be risk-averse, which will be difficult to change as DoD responds to emerging threats and seeks to spur innovation.

Contents

Figures and Tables

Figures

Tables

CHAPTER 1

Background and Context

The U.S. Department of Defense's (DoD's) Planning, Programming, Budgeting, and Execution (PPBE) System was first developed in the 1960s as a structured approach for planning long-term resource development, assessing program cost-effectiveness, and aligning resources to strategies. Over the years, changes to the strategic environment, the industrial base, and the nature of military capabilities have raised the question of whether DoD budgeting processes remain well aligned with national security needs.

Congress, in the National Defense Authorization Act for Fiscal Year 2022, called for the establishment of a Commission on PPBE Reform.[1] To fulfill the goals set out by Congress, the commission is conducting a review of lessons from the PPBE-like systems of comparative organizations to improve DoD's PPBE System.

As part of this data collection, the commission asked the National Defense Research Institute, a federally funded research and development center operated by the RAND National Security Research Division, to conduct case studies of budgeting processes across nine comparative organizations: five international defense organizations and four U.S. federal government agencies. Congress also specifically requested two case studies of near-peer competitors, and we selected the additional seven cases in close partnership with the commission. The commission will use insights from these analyses to derive potential lessons for DoD on PPBE reform and convey its recommendations to Congress.

This report is Volume 4 in a four-volume set, three of which present case studies conducted in support of the Commission on PPBE Reform. The accompanying volumes focus on selected near-peer competitors (*Planning, Programming, Budgeting, and Execution in Comparative Organizations:* Vol. 1, *Case Studies of China and Russia*), selected U.S. partners and allies (*Planning, Programming, Budgeting, and Execution in Comparative Organizations:* Vol. 2, *Case Studies of Selected Allied and Partner Nations*), and comparable U.S. federal government agencies (*Planning, Programming, Budgeting, and Execution in Comparative Organizations:* Vol. 3, *Case Studies of Selected Non-DoD Federal Agencies*).[2] This volume, an executive summary, distills key insights from these three analytical volumes.

---

[1] Public Law 117-81, National Defense Authorization Act for Fiscal Year 2022, December 27, 2021.

[2] Megan McKernan, Stephanie Young, Timothy R. Heath, Dara Massicot, Mark Stalczynski, Ivana Ke, Raphael S. Cohen, John P. Godges, Heidi Peters, and Lauren Skrabala, *Planning, Programming, Budgeting, and Execution in Comparative Organizations:* Vol. 1, *Case Studies of China and Russia*, RAND Corporation,

Methodology, Limitations, and Caveats

We built our case studies and analyses on five methodological foundations:

- We formed diverse interdisciplinary teams that drew on staff from RAND's U.S. offices, RAND Europe, and RAND Australia, who had direct experience with the comparative organizations that were the focus of the case studies detailed in the three companion volumes of this report series.
- Acting on guidance from the commission, we developed and used a case-study template and interview protocol to ensure a systematic approach to all the case studies and to facilitate comparisons.
- Literature reviews were extensive and included government documents on budget processes and policies, published academic research, trade literature, and research by international organizations.
- Foreign-language proficiency among the research staff ensured that we could analyze foreign-language sources relevant to the China and Russia case studies.
- We held more than 100 structured discussions with subject-matter experts and practitioners, including budget officials; staff from the offices of chief financial officers; programmers; and experts from academia, federally funded research and development centers, and think tanks.

All nine case studies entailed extensive document reviews and structured discussions with subject-matter experts who had experience with the budgeting processes of the international governments and selected U.S. federal government agencies. Each case study was assigned a unique team with appropriate regional or organizational expertise. For the near-peer competitor cases (China and Russia), the assigned experts had the language skills and methodological training to work with primary sources in Chinese or Russian. The analysis was also supplemented by experts in the U.S. PPBE process, as applicable. Finally, the RAND research team was led by two researchers who helped ensure that each case study team had some autonomy while maintaining unity in the overall research approach.

Each case study proceeded in two phases. First, we gathered descriptive content from sources and interviews. Then, we funneled the content into a structured analysis of potential lessons for DoD. Figures 1.1 and 1.2 list the types of information gathered and analyzed in each phase.

RR-A2195-1, 2024; Megan McKernan, Stephanie Young, Andrew Dowse, James Black, Devon Hill, Benjamin J. Sacks, Austin Wyatt, Nicolas Jouan, Yuliya Shokh, Jade Yeung, Raphael S. Cohen, John P. Godges, Heidi Peters, and Lauren Skrabala, *Planning, Programming, Budgeting, and Execution in Comparative Organizations: Vol. 2, Case Studies of Selected Allied and Partner Nations*, RAND Corporation, RR-A2195-2, 2024; Megan McKernan, Stephanie Young, Ryan Consaul, Michael Simpson, Sarah W. Denton, Anthony Vassalo, William Shelton, Devon Hill, Raphael S. Cohen, John P. Godges, Heidi Peters, and Lauren Skrabala, *Planning, Programming, Budgeting, and Execution in Comparative Organizations: Vol. 3, Case Studies of Selected Non-DoD Federal Agencies*, RAND Corporation, RR-A2195-3, 2024.

FIGURE 1.1

Case-Study Descriptive Content Sought in Data Collection

Overview	Planning and Programming	Budgeting and Execution	Oversight
• **Size and nature** of budget • **Key steps** in resource planning (analogous to PPBE processes), including a flow chart • Extent to which **processes are tailored** to certain functions • Factors informing **why the organization has developed** this approach	• **Key stakeholders and participants**; roles and responsibilities • Data and **information management** processes • **Key decision products** • **Tools**; analytic basis for decisionmaking • Tailored processes **for high-tech investments**	• **Degree of fungibility** of resourcing • Organizational **level at which resource decisions are made** (e.g., program, portfolio) • **Processes for changing** planned resource levels • **Feedback mechanisms** to assess the effectiveness of investments	• **Processes** for legislative review, or other forms of oversight • **Key features of oversight**; timeline, key guidance products, mechanisms for changes, rules governing execution • Mechanisms for **reporting and compliance** • Processes for **financial audits**

FIGURE 1.2

Case-Study Analysis of Lessons for DoD

Analysis	Target Evaluation Criteria	Insights to Inform DoD's PPBE Process
• **Strengths and weaknesses**, e.g., relative to efficiency, life-cycle planning, flexibility, efficacy of oversights • **Areas for potential U.S. competitive advantage or disadvantage**, relative to adversaries • **Generalizability or applicability** of lessons from each case to other circumstances	• **Thoughtful and responsible use** of resources • **Value to the warfighter** (i.e., does process meet mission needs?) • **Plans linked to budgets** • **Sustained funding** for long-term initiatives • **Flexibility** in case of emerging requirements • Proper **oversight** (or does the process risk misuse of funds?)	• **Lessons for DoD from each case** regarding PPBE • Insights for DoD on how **adversary processes could affect U.S. competitive advantage** • **Caveats and cautions** to inform interpretation

We faced three notable limitations in conducting this research. First, the work required detailed analyses of nine extraordinarily diverse case studies on the tight timeline required by the commission's challenging congressional mandate. Second, all cases presented challenges of data availability—ranging from the opacity of decisionmaking in the near-peer cases to classification issues to differences between formal documentation and how things actually work. Third, the differences and inconsistencies across the cases made it challenging to conduct assessments of cross-case comparability (or comparability with DoD); the international cases involved unique political cultures, governance structures, strategic concerns, and military commitments; and the U.S. agencies had their own unique missions, cultures, resource levels, and congressional oversight.

In light of these limitations and challenges, any key insights that we derived should be interpreted as perceived strengths, weaknesses, and lessons about an organization in meeting its *own* mission needs. Developing normative judgments about best practices or internally consistent intercase evaluations is extremely difficult, if only because not all the organizations share the same values or priorities.

Organization of This Report

Chapters 2–4 provide overviews of the key insights from the near-peer cases, allied cases, and non-DoD federal agency cases, respectively, as drawn from the three companion volumes in this report series.[3] This high-level review consolidates the perceived strengths, weaknesses, and lessons from the three sets of PPBE-like systems examined. Each chapter on key insights includes a discussion of their possible applicability to DoD. The applicability sections speak directly to the commission's mandate—and to the potential utility for DoD's PPBE System. Finally, in Chapter 5, we provide summary tables for the governance and budgetary systems of the near-peer and allied case studies, along with the budgetary flexibilities of the non-DoD federal cases.

---

[3] These case studies are fully presented in McKernan, Young, Heath, et al., 2024; McKernan, Young, Dowse, et al., 2024; and McKernan, Young, Consaul, et al., 2024.

CHAPTER 2

Key Insights from Case Studies of China and Russia

The key insights from the China and Russia case studies are as follows:

- **China and Russia make top-down decisions about priorities and risks but face limitations in implementation.** Senior leaders in these countries have the authority to make top-down decisions, but realizing returns on those decisions is contingent on key social, economic, and other factors. In China, modernization efforts in such areas as jet engines and semiconductors have not yielded consistent outcomes; other determinative factors are long-term investment stability, innovation enablers, and a workforce with relevant expertise. In Russia, a significant increase in the defense budget for the war in Ukraine, along with the adoption of new mobilization laws, have run into limitations in industrial capacity, supply chain reliability, and the ability to call up required manpower, even through conscription.
- **China and Russia make long-term plans but have mechanisms for changing course in accordance with changing priorities.** Centralized decisionmaking in both countries can reduce the friction associated with course corrections, but China is less likely than Russia to face hard choices when it comes to reprioritizing because of China's economic growth over recent decades.
- **Especially in China, political leaders provide stable and sustained long-term support for military modernization priorities.** The lack of political opposition, the high degree of alignment between military and senior political leaders, and the sheer scale of military investment over several decades have facilitated the stable planning and long-term investments that are essential for making progress toward complex modernization priorities. In contrast, Russia has a ten-year armaments program supported by a three-year budget—a combination that, in theory, balances stability with flexibility. But, in reality, the three-year budget is aspirational and has been rapidly jettisoned without political or legal blowback, leaving defense industrial base companies in a vulnerable position over the long term.
- **China and Russia have weak mechanisms for avoiding graft and ensuring transparency, efficiency, effectiveness, and quality control in PPBE-like processes.** The power dynamics and the structures of decisionmaking in these countries provide lim-

ited guardrails for ensuring the efficiency, effectiveness, and oversight of investments. China's budgeting processes are hampered by clientelism (bribery), patronage (favoritism), and other forms of corruption that pervade the defense industries. China's authorities also regard their budget processes as lagging those of Western counterparts. Powerful state-owned enterprises continue to operate in a highly inefficient and wasteful manner, partly because of the political power they exert. Similarly, in Russia, defense spending is subject to corruption in the Ministry of Defense, cronyism throughout the defense industrial base, and a general lack of serious anticorruption measures.

- **Reforms in China and Russia have been designed to increase the oversight of resource allocation processes.** China, since at least the early 2000s, and Russia, since the 2020s, have recognized the inefficiencies and limited avenues for competing voices in their top-down budget processes. They have looked to other international models, including those used in the United States, for lessons on budget reforms. In accordance with centrally directed reforms, the People's Liberation Army has carried out multiple rounds of reforms in its budgeting and financial system. Chinese leaders have long recognized that the military's budget system, like that of the government overall, suffers from severe problems related to corruption and weak accountability. The Russian budget is based on best practices, such as the use of a three-year or medium-term expenditure framework, and prior to the invasion of Ukraine, fiscally conservative funding was allocated annually within reasonable constraints. Nonetheless, budget execution in Russia has few safeguards, little oversight, and meager quality control.

Applicability of Insights from Case Studies of China and Russia

Although the 2022 National Defense Strategy calls out China and Russia as posing particular challenges to the United States and the international order, the nature of those challenges are distinct and situationally dependent. China and Russia have unique histories, economic conditions, industrial capacities, and military capabilities; thus, they pose separate challenges to the United States. Societal fundamentals for building military capability are critical factors in determining the success of military modernization; thus, it is unclear how much success can be meaningfully attributed to resource planning processes. Additional critical inputs to success include the following:

- workforce capacity, capabilities, and productivity
- the scale and focus of defense investment over time
- industrial capacity and capability
- industrial policy
- innovation policy.

China and Russia are also both extraordinarily different from the United States in terms of their political cultures, governance structures, and strategic orientations. Both have demonstrated that strong central authority can ensure that long-term planning (without opposition) aligns resources to priorities, and these countries are able to redirect resources to meet changing needs. However, there are constraints and trade-offs that come with a top-down approach. For example, it can hamper innovation and yield weak mechanisms for oversight and quality control of budget execution.

Given this context, the lessons for U.S. PPBE reform efforts cannot be directly applicable. In addition, there is immense information asymmetry: It is difficult to gain a complete picture of China's and Russia's budgetary processes from open-source reporting—in contrast to the abundance of open-source critiques of U.S. PPBE processes. The risk is that China's and Russia's processes may sound more ideal because of the lack of publicly available information about their execution. Despite these differences, the case studies suggest several considerations that are relevant for the United States.

The Commission on PPBE Reform is looking for potential lessons from the PPBE-like systems of competitor nations to improve DoD's PPBE System. The relevance of these lessons—particularly from China—will invariably be constrained by the differences in the U.S. political system.

DoD likely will not find a simple way of replicating Chinese advantages by imitation, given the stark differences between the U.S. and Chinese governmental systems. However, finding analogous measures to achieve similar effects could be worthwhile. In particular, two types of measures could be beneficial for DoD budgeting practices: (1) finding ways to ensure sustained, consistent funding for priority projects over many years; and (2) delegating more authority and granting greater flexibility to project and program managers, without compromising accountability, so that they can make changes to stay in alignment with guidance as technologies and programs advance.

Russia can be fiscally conservative at the federal level, and its defense acquisition plans are often closely tied to military strategy and defense needs. However, opacity in multiple parts of Russia's PPBE-like process often perpetuates corruption and generates outputs of varying quality from the country's defense industry. The Russian system does not allow sufficient oversight to ensure that it works effectively or produces uniformly high-quality products.

Despite the frequent public discussion in the United States that oversight adds time to DoD's PPBE processes, it is clear from the Chinese and Russian experiences that oversight is a critical element that ultimately helps in the successful deployment of capabilities for use in operations and, therefore, should not be haphazardly traded away for speed during resource allocation.

CHAPTER 3

Key Insights from Case Studies of Allied and Partner Nations

The key insights from the case studies of selected allied and partner nations—Australia, Canada, and the United Kingdom (UK)—are as follows:

- **Australia, Canada, and the UK have a shared commitment to democratic political institutions with the United States and converge on a similar strategic vision.** This alignment not only presents opportunities for co-development and broader prospects for working together toward shared goals but also requires the United States and its allies and partners to develop more-effective partnership approaches. In addition, each country struggles to balance the needs to keep pace with strategic threats, execute longer-term plans, use deliberate processes with sufficient oversight, and encourage innovation.
- **Foreign military sales are important mechanisms for strategic convergence but pose myriad challenges for coordination and resource planning.** Australia, Canada, and the UK rely on U.S. foreign military sales to promote strategic convergence, interconnectedness, interoperability, interchangeability, and the shared benefits of innovation. One downside to this reliance is that exchange-rate volatility can require unexpected budget adjustments.[1] Another downside is less ability for each country to independently act with flexibility.
- **The Australian, Canadian, and UK political systems shape the roles and contours of resource planning.** In all three countries, the executive branch has the power of the purse, which reduces political friction over appropriations.
- **Australia, Canada, and the UK have less legislative intervention in budgeting processes, relative to the United States, and do not need to confront the challenges of operating without a regular appropriation (as is the case under continuing resolutions).** These countries' resource management systems have less partisan interference than the United States' system, according to subject-matter experts.

---

[1] Although, in the case of Australia, the government supplements the Department of Defence for exchange rate losses. Additionally, we note that exchange rate fluctuations can be a challenge for any international purchase, not just in the case of reliance on FMS.

- **Strategic planning mechanisms in Australia, Canada, and the UK harness defense spending priorities and drive budget execution.** Each country starts its defense resource management process with strategic planning to identify key priorities for finite funds in defense budgets that are smaller than that of the United States.
- **Jointness in resource planning appears to be easier in Australia, Canada, and the UK, given the smaller size and structure of their militaries.** In each country, there is a greater level of joint financial governance than in the United States, with less focus on service-centric views and more focus on cross-governmental mechanisms and joint funds.
- **Australia, Canada, and the UK place a greater emphasis on budget predictability and stability than on agility.** Australia's Department of Defence is assured of sustained funding for four years and plans investments as far as 20 years out. The notional budget of Canada's Department of National Defence is guaranteed to continue year on year, and the department's Capital Investment Fund ensures that approved projects are paid for years or even decades in advance. UK Ministry of Defence programs are normally guaranteed funding for three to five years, with estimates out to ten years. In contrast, Congress must revisit and vote on DoD's entire budget every year.
- **Despite the common emphasis on stability, each system provides some budget flexibility to address unanticipated changes.** The Australian Parliament can boost the defense budget in periods of national emergency or to fund overseas military operations, and the government can supplement defense allocations to alleviate inflationary pressures. In Canada, regular supplementary parliamentary spending periods can help close unforeseen defense funding gaps. The UK Ministry of Defence has mechanisms for moving money between accounts (e.g., a process known as *virement* for reallocating funds with either Treasury or parliamentary approval, depending on the circumstances) and accessing additional funds in a given fiscal year (FY).
- **Similar budget mechanisms are used in Australia, Canada, and the UK.** All three countries carry over funds, move funds across portfolios, appropriate funds with different expirations, and supplement funds for emerging needs. The use of these mechanisms, however, varies across the cases.
- **Australia, Canada, and the UK have all pivoted toward supporting agility and innovation in the face of lengthy acquisition cycles.** The proposed Australian Strategic Capabilities Accelerator would be required to move funds between projects to accelerate innovation. Canada, whose strategic plan calls for its Department of National Defence to exploit defense innovation,[2] is partnering with the United States to modernize the North American Aerospace Defense Command (NORAD). Like DoD, the UK Ministry of Defence is experimenting with ways to encourage innovation, including a new Inno-

---

[2] Canadian Department of National Defence, *Department of National Defence and Canadian Armed Forces, 2022–2023: Departmental Plan*, 2022.

vation Fund, which allows the chief scientific adviser to pursue higher-risk projects as part of the primary research and development budget.

- **Australia, Canada, and the UK have independent oversight functions for ensuring the transparency, audits, or contestability of budgeting processes.** Accountability in Australia is provided through the Australian National Audit Office, the Portfolio Budget Statement, the contestability function, and other reviews. Parliamentary oversight—or scrutiny—in Canada is aided by analyses from the Auditor General, the Parliamentary Budget Officer, and at times the Library of Parliament. Each year, the UK Ministry of Defence budget is externally vetted by the House of Commons Public Accounts Committee, UK National Audit Office, and the Comptroller and Auditor General to ensure that funds are not misused.

- **Despite the push to accept additional risk, there is still a cultural aversion to risk in the Australian, Canadian, and British budgeting processes.** In Australia, stakeholders seek to spend within annual budget limits, which is intuitively prudent but could limit agility by lengthening review times and holding up funds for other projects. Canada's political structure does not allow parliament to drastically change funding for departments, including the Department of National Defence, beyond what has been requested. The experiments by the UK Ministry of Defence to encourage innovation have not made its culture less risk-averse.

Applicability of Insights from Case Studies of Allied and Partner Nations

Of particular concern for DoD is its yearly vulnerability to political gridlock, continuing resolutions, and potential government shutdowns—all of which are obstacles that allies and partners do not endure. Without altering the U.S. system of government, which deliberately empowers strong voices from both the executive and legislative branches in defense budget decisionmaking, the United States could learn from allied and partner budgetary mechanisms that provide extra budget surety for major multiyear investments without requiring their reevaluation every year.

For example, the UK defense budgeting system benefits from multiannual spending plans, programs, and contracts. The Ministry of Defence can sign decade-long portfolio management agreements with UK firms to provide long-term certainty. The UK system also allows for advance funding early in a budget year to ensure continuous government operations, thereby avoiding the possibility—and cost—of a shutdown. Likewise, Australia's defense budgeting processes provide a high level of certainty for the development and operationalization of major military capabilities. These farsighted processes strengthen the link between strategy and resources, reduce the prospects for misused funds or inefficiency, and limit the risk of blocked funding from year to year.

CHAPTER 4

Key Insights from Case Studies of Non-DoD Federal Agencies

The key insights from the case studies of selected non-DoD federal agencies—the U.S. Department of Homeland Security (DHS), the U.S. Department of Health and Human Services (HHS), the National Aeronautics and Space Administration (NASA), and the Office of the Director of National Intelligence (ODNI)—are as follows:

- **Other U.S. government agencies looked to DoD's PPBE System as a model in developing their own systems, which subsequently evolved.** NASA's PPBE, ODNI's Intelligence Planning, Programming, Budgeting, and Evaluation (IPPBE), DHS's PPBE, and HHS's budget process all refer to DoD's PPBE System as a model for planning and resource allocation decisionmaking. However, these agencies' budget processes have evolved differently in accordance with their missions, organizational structures, authorities, staff capacities, available resources, and many other factors. One notable and deliberate difference between ODNI's IPPBE and DoD's PPBE processes is ODNI's substitution of *evaluation* for DoD's *execution* in ODNI's definition of the term. Despite the evolution away from DoD's PPBE framework, all four agencies still generally follow a budgeting process that is common to most U.S. federal civilian agencies. This process begins with an annual planning cycle and culminates in budget execution and performance evaluation.
- **Long-term planning is often limited relative to that done by DoD.** One difference between DoD and three of the agencies that we examined is DoD's focus on long-term planning processes. We attribute this difference both to the inherently dynamic requirements of the DHS and HHS mission sets and to the weaker (relative to DoD) mechanisms for forging forward-looking, cross-departmental plans through a headquarters function in DHS and ODNI. Long-term planning is particularly important for agencies with missions that require sustained development efforts rather than short-term operational programs.
- **A variety of mechanisms enable budget flexibility and agility.** Mechanisms have been designed to meet dynamic mission demands, highly variable mission needs, and emerging public health threats. Other mechanisms have given agencies more discretion (than in DoD) to redirect appropriated funds without reporting to Congress. HHS appears to

have wide latitude in how appropriated funds are spent. Unlike DoD, NASA does not appear to receive appropriations in distinct titles. Various mechanisms allow the agencies to carry over partial funding across years, repurpose expiring unobligated balances, and reallocate funds to department-wide capital investments. In some instances, Congress further enables agility by employing broader appropriation categories than those used for DoD appropriations; in this way, agency decisionmakers have more flexibility to implement changes to previously communicated funding priorities.

- **Mechanisms for enabling agility help agencies weather continuing resolutions and other sources of budget turbulence.** Budget flexibility can also help an agency sustain its operations under continuing resolutions. NASA's two-year expiration timeline for appropriations reportedly provides the agency with a cushion in the likely event that a regular appropriation is delayed. HHS develops requests for grant proposals ahead of anticipated continuing resolutions. The ability of DHS components to carry over up to 50 percent of prior-year balances into the next FY could help the agency mitigate the effects of continuing resolutions. Most mandatory HHS programs, such as Medicare and children's entitlement programs, are budgeted on ten-year schedules outside the annual appropriations process and, thus, are rarely subject to continuing resolutions.

- **The latest replacement of execution with evaluation in PPBE-like processes could be instructive for DoD.** ODNI is not alone in substituting *evaluation* for *execution* in the name of its budgeting process. DHS has essentially done so in its PPBE-like process to better track the results of its spending: The department now issues annual evaluation plans. This line of effort demonstrates an investment by DHS in evaluation activities. DHS's efforts in this area could inform DoD's approach to the execution phase.

- **Implementation of PPBE-like processes at the scale of DoD's process is resource-intensive, institutionally challenging, and often infeasible for smaller agencies.** One area in which the selected non-DoD agencies cannot emulate an exemplary DoD PPBE capability is DoD's Cost Assessment and Program Evaluation (CAPE) analytic function. In these four agencies, there is no CAPE-like function of comparable size and mission because this function is resource-intensive to build and maintain and would be challenging to empower institutionally. CAPE's mission is to provide DoD with unbiased analysis to support resource allocation. By comparison, NASA's planning, programming, and budgeting are handled within one organization, which may not be considered independent when it scrutinizes NASA's budget submissions. ODNI attempted to emulate the analytic rigor of the CAPE function but found it difficult to do so.

- **Consolidated resource management information systems could improve visibility across the federated structures of government agencies.** DHS's consolidation of its PPBE information system has enhanced its ability to create and manage budgets. DHS officials report that the agency's consolidated system for generating congressional budget justification documents, developing a five-year funding plan, and capturing performance management data has reduced its reliance on Microsoft Excel spreadsheet templates and data reentry, allowing DHS to automate the generation of certain reports that were previously created manually. In contrast, the lack of a consolidated budget formulation system has left HHS leadership with limited visibility into the department's operating division budgets. DoD could examine the feasibility of implementing a consolidated PPBE information system and whether the benefits of doing so would outweigh the costs.

Applicability of Insights from Case Studies of Non-DoD Federal Agencies

Although the budgeting processes of the non-DoD federal agencies that we examined were originally modeled after DoD's PPBE System, these processes have been adapted to the unique missions of each agency. Despite moving away from DoD's PPBE model, the agencies still use similar processes. For this reason, there would be no benefit to DoD in adopting any of these systems wholesale. However, there is value in exploring how Congress provides each agency with flexibility so that DoD can ask for similar support that can help it spur innovation, make funding more predictable over multiple years, and obtain relief from various pain points in the system. These pain points include continuing resolutions, rigid appropriations categories, and appropriations for line items instead of portfolios. The Commission on PPBE Reform could further explore the mechanisms discussed in the following sections for flexibility.

Flexibility in DHS Processes

DHS funds are typically budgeted annually, but some programs receive multiyear or no-year appropriations. Congress sometimes appropriates multiyear funds to major acquisition programs to foster a stable production and contracting environment. A key example of no-year money is the Disaster Relief Fund, which is meant to give the Federal Emergency Management Agency the flexibility to respond quickly to emerging disaster relief and recovery needs. As another example, in our interviews, DHS officials mentioned how the department's border security, fencing, infrastructure, and technology appropriation gave it the ability to carry over significant amounts of funds related to this mission area. (DHS officials noted that funds are no longer appropriated to this account and that the use of no-year appropriations was significantly curtailed with the implementation of the common appropriations structure.) Congress also authorizes DHS components to carry over one-year operations and support accounts into the next FY and to expend up to 50 percent of the prior-year lapsed balance amounts. Beyond the base budget, DHS often receives supplemental funds for emergent requirements; the number of requirements varies from year to year.

Flexibility in HHS Processes

HHS has access to emergency supplemental funding and several flexible-spending accounts, such as the Nonrecurring Expenses Fund, which allows HHS to reallocate expired, unobligated funds to capital investments. These flexibility mechanisms are often given multiyear or no-year funding. HHS does not use a common appropriations structure, so budget justifications focus heavily on missions and needs. This focus allows the operating divisions and department-level leadership on the Secretary's Budget Council to concentrate on aligning program budgets and missions with the Secretary's priorities.

Flexibility in NASA Processes

NASA requests and is allocated funding differently from DoD. Because NASA's funds are appropriated to mission directorates primarily at the mission, theme, and project levels, NASA has some flexibility to align project funding to meet changing priorities or real-world circumstances. Our review of NASA's FY 2023 congressional justification indicates that it does not request—nor is it funded with—appropriations split into categories, such as research, development, test, and evaluation (RDT&E); procurement; and operation and maintenance in the same manner as DoD, and this was confirmed during our interviews. Therefore, NASA does not appear to encounter the same types of restrictions as DoD with respect to using specific funding for specific activities (e.g., using RDT&E only during the design and development stages of a program). Moreover, all of NASA's appropriations, except for construction, have two-year durations. NASA has obligation goals of 90–95 percent in the first year of two-year funds, which allows for some funding to be expended in the second year, typically at the start of the FY. Given that continuing resolutions are a real possibility, this carryover funding can mitigate many shortfalls that might result at the start of an FY—and thus act as a cushion for continuing resolutions, although that has not been the primary intention for the authority to carry forward funds.

Flexibility in ODNI Processes

ODNI funds may be reprogrammed under five conditions: (1) when funds are transferred to a high-priority intelligence activity in support of an emergent need, (2) when funds are not moved to a reserve for contingencies by the Director of National Intelligence or Central Intelligence Agency, (3) when funds are cumulatively less than $150 million and less than 5 percent of the annual accounts available to a department or agency, (4) when the action does not terminate an acquisition program, and (5) when the congressional notification period is satisfied. Congress must be notified of above-the-threshold reprogramming actions (i.e., those that exceed $150 million or 5 percent of accounts available to a department or agency under the National Intelligence Program in a single FY) within 30 days, or 15 days for matters of urgent national security concern. Below-the-threshold reprogramming actions do not require congressional notification. However, ODNI does notify Congress of below-the-threshold actions that may be of congressional interest.

CHAPTER 5

Summary of Cross-Case Insights

Summary of Defense Governance and Budgetary Systems of U.S. and Comparative Nations

In Tables 5.1 through 5.10, we summarize the defense governance and budgetary systems of the assessed near-peer, allied, and partner nations, compared with U.S. defense governance and budgetary systems. These tables are organized first by governance systems (Tables 5.1 and 5.2) and then by the four budgetary functions of planning (Tables 5.3 and 5.4), programming (Tables 5.5 and 5.6), budgeting (Tables 5.7 and 5.8), and execution (Tables 5.9 and 5.10).[1]

TABLE 5.1

Governance: U.S. and Comparative Nation Government Structures and Key Participants

Country	Structure of Government or Political System	Key Governing Bodies and Participants
United States	Federal presidential constitutional republic	• President of the United States • Office of Management and Budget (OMB) • Congress (House of Representatives and Senate) • U.S. Department of Defense (DoD) • Secretary of Defense and senior DoD leadership • Joint Chiefs of Staff
China	Unitary one-party socialist republic	• Politburo Standing Committee • National People's Congress (NPC) • Central Military Commission (CMC)
Russia	Federal semi-presidential republic	• President of Russia • Federal Assembly (State Duma and the Federation Council) • President's Security Council • Ministry of Defense (MoD) • Military-Industrial Commission (VPK) • Rostec (Russian state-owned defense conglomerate headquartered in Moscow)
Australia	Federal parliamentary constitutional monarchy	• Prime minister • Governor-general • Parliament (House of Representatives and Senate) • Minister for Defence • Department of Defence

---

[1] Information in these tables is derived from multiple sources cited in McKernan, Young, Heath, et al., 2024; and McKernan, Young, Dowse, et al., 2024.

Table 5.1—Continued

Country	Structure of Government or Political System	Key Governing Bodies and Participants
Canada	Federal parliamentary constitutional monarchy	• Prime minister • Governor general • Parliament (House of Commons and Senate) • Department of National Defence • Minister of Finance • Minister of National Defence • Deputy Minister of National Defence
UK	Unitary parliamentary constitutional monarchy	• Prime minister • Parliament (House of Commons and House of Lords) • Ministry of Defence (MoD) • Secretary of State for Defence • Permanent Under-Secretary of State for Defence

TABLE 5.2

Governance: U.S. and Comparative Nation Spending Controls and Decision Support Systems

Country	Control of Government Spending	Decision Support Systems
United States	Legislative review and approval of executive budget proposal	• Planning, Programming, Budgeting, and Execution (PPBE) System • Joint Capabilities Integration and Development System (JCIDS) • Defense Acquisition System (DAS)
China	Executive with nominal legislative review and approval	• 2019 Defense White Paper indicated adoption of "demand-oriented planning" and "planning-led" resource allocation
Russia	Executive with assessed nominal legislative review and approval	• Unclear
Australia	Executive with legislative review and approval. Appropriations legislation must originate in the House of Representatives; Senate may reject legislation but cannot amend it.	One Defense Capability System (ODCS), including the following: • the Integrated Force Design Process, featuring a two-year cycling Defense Capability Assessment Program (DCAP) • the Integrated Investment Program (IIP), which documents planned future capability investments and informs the Portfolio Budget Statement, the proposed allocation of resources to outcomes • acquisition of approved IIP capability programs • sustainment and disposal of capability programs.
Canada	Executive with assessed limited influence of legislative review and approval	• Expenditure Management System • Defence Capabilities Board • Independent Review Panel for Defence Acquisition
UK	Executive with legislative review and approval	• Public Finance Management Cycle • Planning, Budgeting, and Forecasting (PB&F) • Defence Operating Model

TABLE 5.3

Planning: U.S. and Comparative Nation Inputs and Outputs

Country	Key Planning Inputs	Selected Planning Outputs
United States	• National Security Strategy • National Defense Strategy • National Military Strategy	• Chairman's Program Recommendations • Defense Planning Guidance • Fiscal Guidance
China	• Five-Year Programs • Military Strategic Guidelines • Other multiyear plans (People's Liberation Army [PLA] five-year professional development plans, etc.) • Annual PLA budget requirements	• Outline of the Five-Year Program for Military Development • Military components of other multiyear plans • Annual PLA budgets
Russia	• State Armaments Program (SAP) procurement plan	• State Defense Order (SDO)
Australia	• 2016 Defence White Paper • 2017 Defence Industry Policy Statement • 2017 Strategy Framework • 2019 Defence Policy for Industry Participation • 2020 Defence Strategic Update • 2020 Force Structure Plan • 2023 Defence Strategic Review • Defence Planning Guidance/Chief of the Defence Force Preparedness Directive (Not available to the general public) • Other strategic plans and documents outlining planning and program requirements	• IIP for future capability investment
Canada	• 2017 defence white paper (*Strong, Secure, Engaged*) • 2018 Defence Plan, 2018–2023 • 2019 Defence Investment Plan • 2020 Defence Capabilities Blueprint (updated monthly) • 2022 Department of National Defence and Canadian Armed Forces Engagement Plan (released annually)	• Annual department plans to link Department of National Defence (DND) strategic priorities and expected program results to the Main Estimates presented to parliament
UK	• Public Finance Management Cycle • PB&F • Defence Operating Model	• 2021 Defence Command Paper (*Defence in a Competitive Age*) aligns MoD priorities with the Integrated Review • 2021 Defence and Security Industrial Strategy

TABLE 5.4

Planning: U.S. and Comparative Nation Strategic Emphasis and Stakeholders

Country	Strategic Planning Emphasis	Planning Stakeholders
United States	2022 National Defense Strategy highlights four priorities: (1) defending the United States, "paced to the growing multi-domain threat posed by the PRC"; (2) deterring "strategic attacks against the United States, Allies, and partners"; (3) deterring aggression and being prepared to "prevail in conflict when necessary," with priority placed first on the People's Republic of China "challenge in the Indo-Pacific region" and then "the Russia challenge in Europe"; and (4) "building a resilient Joint Force and defense ecosystem."	• Under Secretary of Defense for Policy (lead actor, produces Defense Planning Guidance) • President (National Security Strategy, Fiscal Guidance) • Secretary of Defense (National Defense Strategy, Fiscal Guidance at DoD level) • Chairman of the Joint Chiefs of Staff (CJCS) (National Military Strategy, Chairman's Program Recommendations)
China	Focused, long-term investment for priority projects of high strategic value	• Central Chinese Communist Party leadership • National People's Congress • State Council • Defense-related state-owned enterprises • CMC, senior military leadership
Russia	Closely linked to strategy and national security threats with a recent emphasis on modernization; assessed to be, in part, aspirational	• MoD • Central Research Institute • VPK, representing Rostec, defense industry, and national security agencies
Australia	2023 Defence Strategic Review emphasized a strategy of deterrence to deny an adversary freedom of action to militarily coerce Australia and to operate against Australia without being held at risk	• Strategic guidance generated by Department of Defence; approved by the Minister for Defence • IIP managed by the Vice Chief of the Defence Force, with input from stakeholders and joint strategic planning units, such as the Force Design Division
Canada	2017 white paper emphasized three components of Canadian national defense: (1) defense of national sovereignty through Canadian Armed Forces capable of assisting in response to natural disasters, search and rescue, and other emergencies; (2) defense of North America through partnership with the United States in NORAD; and (3) international engagements, including through peace support operations and peacekeeping.	• DND and supporting cabinet entities
UK	2021 Defence Command Paper emphasized seven primary goals of the MoD and the British Armed Forces: (1) defense of the UK and its overseas territories, (2) sustainment of UK nuclear deterrence capacity, (3) global influence projection, (4) execution of NATO (North Atlantic Treaty Organization) responsibilities, (5) promotion of national prosperity, (6) peacekeeping contributions, and (7) supporting defense and intelligence-gathering capabilities of UK allies and partners.	• Prime minister's Cabinet Office (Integrated Review) • MoD (Defense Command Paper and other strategic documents)

TABLE 5.5

Programming: U.S. and Comparative Nation Resource Allocations and Time Frames

Country	Resource Allocation Decisions	Programming Time Frame
United States	Documented in Program Objective Memorandum (POM) developed by DoD components, reflecting a "systematic analysis of missions and objectives to be achieved, alternative methods of accomplishing them, and the effective allocation of the resources," and reviewed by the Director of Cost Assessment and Program Evaluation (CAPE)	• 5 years
China	Top-down planning from CMC services and commands supplemented by bottom-up requirements submitted by military unit financial departments	• 5 years, sometimes longer
Russia	Top-down planning from Ministry of Defense for the SDO, the annual appropriation for military procurement to meet the requirements of the SAP	• 3 years; nominal 10-year SAP, revised within 5 years in practice
Australia	Portfolio Budget Statement (as informed by the IIP) for the current fiscal year	Three-tiered funding stream that provides • current fiscal year funding • forward-looking estimates with a high degree of confidence for the next 3 fiscal years • provisional funding with a medium degree of confidence for the next 10 years, as articulated in the IIP and defense strategic guidance documents.
Canada	Government Expenditure Plan and Main Estimates allocate budget resources to departments and programs.	• 3 years, as articulated in the Annual Department Plan
UK	• Main supply estimates (MEs) for the current FY, based on spending limits set in Integrated Review, and additional estimates for 10 years out as articulated in the MoD *Defence Equipment Plan*, which is updated annually • Supplementary supply estimates (SEs) allow MoD to request additional resources, capital, or cash for the current fiscal year. • Excess votes—although discouraged—allow retroactive approval of overruns from a prior fiscal year, because government departments cannot legally spend more money than has been approved by parliament.	• 3–5 years, as articulated in the Integrated Review, which provides medium-term financial planning

TABLE 5.6

Programming: U.S. and Comparative Nation Stakeholders

Country	Programming Stakeholders
United States	• Director, CAPE (lead actor, provides analytic baseline to analyze the POM produced by DoD components, leads program reviews, forecasts resource requirements, and updates the Future Years Defense Program [FYDP]) • DoD components (produce POM, document proposed resource requirements for programs over 5-year timespan, which comprises the FYDP) • CJCS (assesses component POMs, provides chairman's program assessment reflecting the extent to which the military departments [MILDEPs] have satisfied combatant command [COCOM] requirements) • Deputy Secretary of Defense (adjudicates disputes through the Deputy's Management Action Groups) • Secretary of Defense (as needed, directs DoD components to execute Resource Management Decision memorandums to reflect decisionmaking during the programming and budget phases)
China	• Ministry of Finance National Defense Department • CMC Logistics Support Department • CMC Strategic Planning Office
Russia	• Ministry of Finance • Ministry of Economic Development • MoD • President's Security Council • VPK
Australia	• At Department of Defence level, decisionmaking for resources made through Defence Committee (Defence Secretary, Chief of the Defence Force, Vice Chief of the Defence Force, Associate Defence Secretary, Chief Finance Officer) • Capability-related submissions reviewed by Minister for Finance–led National Security Investment Committee of Cabinet • Approved by National Security Committee (prime minister, deputy prime minister, Minister for Defence, Treasurer, Minister for Finance, other ministers when necessary)
Canada	• Treasury Board and Department of Finance (sets annual spending limits for federal agencies that are applicable to capital expenditures and determines the number of new projects funded) • Department of Finance, led by the Minister of Finance (drafts budget for presentation to parliament) • Minister of Finance and prime minister have approval authority. • Assistant Deputy Minister for Finance, DND and the DND Finance Group (prepares DND budget and liaises with Treasury Board Secretariat, Department of Finance, and other federal agencies) • Military service comptrollers
UK	• Component entities negotiate with MoD through "demand" signals; components program against required outputs. • MoD reviews and prioritizes proposed programs through a centralized process. • MoD Director General, Finance, working with the Deputy Chief of the Defense Staff for Military Capability (part of the MoD Financial and Military Capability team) • Supported by Director of Financial Planning and Scrutiny and the Assistant Chief of the Defence Staff for Capability and Force Design (part of the Financial and Military Capability team) • Process execution delegated to the Head of Defence Resources

TABLE 5.7

Budgeting: U.S. and Comparative Nation Time Frames and Major Categories

Country	Budget Approval Time Frames	Major Budget Categories
United States	Annual	• 5 categories: Military Personnel (MILPERS); Operation and Maintenance (O&M); Procurement; Research, Development, Test, and Evaluation (RDT&E); and Military Construction (MILCON)
China	Annual	• 3 reported categories in defense white papers: personnel, armaments, and maintenance and operations
Russia	Annual	• 9 categories: Armed Forces of the Russian Federation, Modernization of the Armed Forces, Mobilization and Pre-Conscription Training, Mobilization of the Economy, Participation in Collective Peacekeeping Agreements, Nuclear Weapons Complex, International Military-Technical Cooperation, Research and Development, and a category designated for Other Expenditures
Australia	• Annual, with separate appropriations bills for existing services and programs and for new programs • Accrual budgeting with budget request covering ongoing costs; associated funding cannot be carried over to the next fiscal year	• 5 categories: Workforce, Operations, Capability Acquisition Programs (including research and development), Capability Sustainment, and Operating Costs
Canada	Annual; disbursement of funds is made through 3 supply periods, each reviewed and approved by parliament with Main Estimates and Supplementary Estimate A (i.e., spending not ready to be included in a Main Estimate at time of preparation) presented in the first supply period. Supplementary Estimate B is presented in the second supply period, and Supplementary Estimate C (as needed) is presented in the third supply period.	• Various categories: votes for separate tranches of funding roughly correspond to DoD's *colors of money*. FY 2022–FY 2023 contained four votes for (1) operating expenditures; (2) capital expenditures, including major capability programs and infrastructure projects; (3) grants and contributions, including payments to NATO and funding for partner-nation military programs; and (4) payments for long-term disability and life insurance plans for Canadian Armed Forces Members. • Main Estimates also categorize spending by purpose. FY 2022–FY 2023 purpose categorizations include such areas as (1) ready forces, (2) capability procurement, (3) future force design, and (4) operations.
UK	Annual	• 8 categories: as split by the MoD for its internal PPBE-like process, corresponding to 8 main MoD organizations, central oversight to promote jointness • Budgets divided into commodity blocks (capital departmental expenditure limit for investment, resource departmental expenditure limit for current costs, etc.) and by activity (personnel, etc.)

TABLE 5.8

Budgeting: Selected U.S. and Comparative Nation Stakeholders

Country	Selected Budgeting Stakeholders
United States	DoD • Under Secretary of Defense (Comptroller) • DoD components and COCOMs Executive branch • OMB Congress • House Budget Committee • Senate Budget Committee • House Appropriations Committee (Defense Subcommittee) • Senate Appropriations Committee (Defense Subcommittee) • House Armed Services Committee • Senate Armed Services Committee
China	• State Council • NPC • NPC Standing Committee • NPC Finance and Economic Committee
Russia	• Ministry of Finance • Ministry of Economic Development • MoD • President • Federal Assembly (State Duma and the Federation Council) • Accounts Chamber
Australia	Department of Defence management • Vice Chief of the Defence Force • Associate Secretary of Defence • Investment Committee (chaired by the Vice Chief of the Defence Force, makes departmental decisions associated with execution of the IIP) • Capability managers (senior military officials, Chief Defence Scientist, CIO, and the Deputy Secretary Security and Estate) and lead delivery groups Decisions are ultimately the responsibility of the civilian executive government (prime minister, cabinet).
Canada	• Treasury Board and Department of Finance • Assistant Deputy Minister for Finance, DND and the DND Finance Group • Military service comptrollers
UK	• His Majesty's (HM) Treasury sets annual limits on net spending. • MoD drafts and presents MEs and SEs to Parliament at different points within FY cycle, in close coordination with HM Treasury. • House of Commons Defence Select Committee examines main supply estimates; Parliament votes on main supply estimates and supplementary supply estimates. • MoD Director General, Finance, working with the Deputy Chief of the Defense Staff for Military Capability (part of the MoD Financial and Military Capability team) • Supported by Director of Financial Planning and Scrutiny and the Assistant Chief of the Defence Staff for Capability and Force Design (part of the Financial and Military Capability team) • Process execution is delegated to the Head of Defence Resources.

TABLE 5.9

Execution: U.S. and Comparative Nation Budgetary Flexibilities and Reprogramming

Country	Budgetary Flexibilities and Reprogramming
United States	• Funding availability varies by account type; multiyear or no-year appropriations for limited programs as authorized by Congress • Limited carryover authority in accordance with OMB Circular A-11 • Reprogramming as authorized; four defined categories of reprogramming actions, including prior-approval reprogramming actions—increasing procurement quantity of a major end item, establishing a new program, etc.—which require approval from congressional defense committees • Transfers as authorized through general and special transfer authorities, typically provided in defense authorization and appropriation acts
China	• Some flexibility extended to lower-level decisionmakers to adjust spending and acquisitions; further specifics unclear
Russia	• Signed contract timelines shorter than SAP timelines; provides some degree of flexibility to MoD to realign procurements with changing strategic goals; further specifics unclear
Australia	• Ten-year indicative baseline for defense spending (except operating costs) provides budgetary certainty entering into each new fiscal year. • IIP includes approved capability development programs—for which funding does not expire—and unapproved programs that can be accelerated or delayed as needs arise or change to reallocate funds through biannual review process overseen by the Vice Chief of the Defence Force, including between services and for new projects • IIP is 20% overprogrammed for acquisition to manage risks of underachievement or overexpenditure relative to the acquisition budget. • Funding for operations, sustainment, and personnel is separate from the IIP. • Capability managers have a high degree of flexibility for spending allocated operating funds; responsible for achieving outcomes articulated in the Portfolio Budget Statement.
Canada	• Organizations can transfer funds within a vote from one program to another without parliament's approval. • Organizations need parliament's approval to transfer funds between votes. • Canadian federal agencies are allowed to carry forward a portion of unspent funds for a fiscal year—typically up to 5% of operating expenditures and 20% of capital expenditures. • Government can authorize continued spending at prior-year levels if a budget has not been passed by parliament by the beginning of the fiscal year. • Special warrants can be issued to fund continued normal government operations if a government falls and an election is called before a budget can be passed; this can also be used on a short-term basis to avoid the need for a parliament vote on funding. • Interim supply bill for a new fiscal year is typically presented and voted on in third supply period of prior fiscal year to allow continued government operations; the budget and Main Estimates are introduced close to the beginning of a new fiscal year.
UK	• Defense operations funded separately through HM Treasury or (in certain circumstances) UK Integrated Security Fund (as managed by the Cabinet Office's) Joint Funds Unit • Already voted funding can be moved within top-line budget programs with HM Treasury approval, provided they remain in the same commodity block • MoD funds can also be directly transferred between programs within a departmental expenditure limit or annual managed expenditure in a process known as *virement*, subject to restrictions. • Additional funding for one or more top-line budget programs can be requested from Parliament as an SE. • Portions of budget subject to highest degree of fluctuation are treated as annual managed expenditures (with operations covered through HM Treasury and/or UK Integrated Security Fund); MoD can request additional funds from HM Treasury to support urgent and unanticipated needs.

TABLE 5.10

Execution: U.S. and Comparative Nation Assessment

Country	Key Stakeholders in Execution Assessment
United States	• Under Secretary of Defense (Comptroller) • DoD component comptrollers and financial managers • Department of the Treasury • Government Accountability Office • OMB • Defense Finance and Accounting Service
China	• Military Expenditure Performance Management system; guideline-driven performance evaluations of military projects • Ministry of Finance Military Accounting System; evaluation using indicators, such as asset-liability ratios
Russia	• MoD • Federal Agency for State Property Management • Accounts Chamber
Australia	• National Audit Office • Finance regulations within Department of Defence and the public service • Defence Finance Policy Framework • Annual Performance Statement; submitted in October of the year following defense appropriation by the prime minister and cabinet • Portfolio Additional Estimates Statement; reflects budget appropriations and changes between budgets
Canada	• Auditor General • Parliamentary Budget Office • DND internal Review Services division
UK	• National Audit Office • Comptroller and Auditor General • HM Treasury (approval required for any MoD expenditure above £600 million, monthly and annual reporting from MoD on actual and forecasted spending, etc.) • House of Commons Public Accounts Committee

Summary of Budgetary Flexibilities of DoD and Comparative U.S. Federal Agencies

In Tables 5.11 through 5.14, we summarize the budgetary flexibilities of the assessed non-DoD U.S. federal agencies, compared with DoD budgetary flexibilities. As an introduction, Table 5.11 specifies each agency's planning and budget system. Table 5.12 summarizes the funding categories and funding availability within each system. Table 5.13 compares the different types of carryover funds and restrictions during continuing resolutions. Table 5.14 focuses on the different kinds of reprogramming, transfers, and supplemental funding available within each system.[2]

---

[2] Information in these tables is derived from multiple sources cited in McKernan, Young, Consaul, et al., 2024.

TABLE 5.11

Planning and Budget Systems of DoD and Comparative U.S. Agencies

Agency	Planning and Budget System
DoD	Planning, Programming, Budgeting, and Execution (PPBE) System
DHS	Future Years Homeland Security Program (FYHSP)
HHS	No direct analog at the department level; operating divisions (OPDIVs) have individual approaches to annual budget planning and formulation
NASA	PPBE System
ODNI	Intelligence Planning, Programming, Budgeting, and Evaluation (IPPBE) System

TABLE 5.12

Funding Categories and Funding Availability for DoD and Comparative U.S. Agencies

Agency	Funding Categories	Funding Availability
DoD	• Discretionary budget includes Military Personnel (MILPERS), Operation and Maintenance (O&M), Procurement, RDT&E, and Military Construction (MILCON) account categories	• Varies by account type; multiyear or no-year appropriations for limited programs as authorized by Congress
DHS	• Discretionary budget includes component-level accounts organized by four common categories • Mandatory funding for some functions, such as Coast Guard benefits • Some activities funded through discretionary fees and collections	• Varies by account type; multiyear or no-year appropriations for certain programs as authorized
HHS	• Discretionary budget organized under 12 OPDIVs • Mandatory funding is ~90% of budget • Some activities funded through discretionary fees	• One-year appropriations for most of discretionary operational budget; multiyear and no-year appropriations for certain programs
NASA	• Discretionary budget with output-oriented appropriations allocated at program level	• Six-year appropriations, construction • Two-year appropriations (except Office of Inspector General and Construction and Environmental Compliance and Restoration), all other account types
ODNI	• Discretionary budget for National Intelligence Program (NIP) activities managed by ODNI • Discretionary budget for Military Intelligence Program (MIP) activities managed through DoD	• Varies by account type; one-year appropriations for ODNI operations

TABLE 5.13

Carryover Funds and Restrictions for DoD and Comparative U.S. Agencies

Agency	Carryover Funds	Restrictions During Continuing Resolutions
DoD	Limited carryover authority in accordance with OMB Circular A-11	Various; no new programs, increases in production rates, etc.
DHS	Authority to carry forward one-year O&S funding into the next FY; can expend up to 50% of prior-year lapsed balance	Various; no new programs, new hiring, or new contract awards for discretionary programs
HHS	Limited carryover authority in accordance with OMB Circular A-11	Various; new contract awards and grants have been suspended for discretionary programs.
NASA	Limited carryover authority in accordance with OMB Circular A-11	Minimal; two-year appropriations and 90–95% obligation goal for first year of availability allow forward funding of contracts.
ODNI	Limited carryover authority in accordance with OMB Circular A-11	Restrictions on ODNI/NIP operations are unclear; MIP operations are subject to restrictions on DoD activities during continuing resolutions.

TABLE 5.14

Reprogramming, Transfers, and Supplements for DoD and Comparative U.S. Agencies

Agency	Reprogramming	Transfers	Supplemental Funding
DoD	• As authorized; four defined categories of reprogramming actions • Prior-approval reprogramming actions—increasing procurement quantity of a major end item, establishing a new program, etc.— require approval from congressional defense committees	As authorized; general and special transfer authorities, typically provided in defense authorization and appropriations acts	Frequent; linked to emerging operational and national security needs
DHS	• As authorized; request to Congress must be made before June 30 if additional support for emerging needs or crises exceeds 10% of original appropriated funding • Restrictions (creation of program, augmentation of funding in excess of $5M or 10%, reduction of funding by ≥10%, etc.) absent notification	As authorized; up to 5% of current FY appropriations may be transferred if appropriations committees are notified at least 30 days in advance; transfer may not represent >10% increase to an individual program except as otherwise specified	Frequent; linked to Disaster Relief Fund for domestic disaster and emergency response and recovery
HHS	• As authorized; no notification below threshold of lesser of $1M or 10% of an account; notification of reprogramming actions above this threshold are required • Notification required above threshold of $500K if reprogramming decreases appropriated funding by >10% or substantially affects program personnel or operations	As authorized; Secretary's One-Percent Transfer General Provision; allows transfer of up to 1% from any account into another account, not to exceed up to 3% of funds previously in account, maximum transfer amount of ~$900M	Frequent; linked to public health crises, hurricane relief, and refugee resettlement support
NASA	• As authorized; reprogramming documents must be submitted if a budget account changes by $500K • Within the Exploration Systems and Space Operations account, no more than 10% of funds for Explorations Systems may be reprogrammed for Space Operations and vice versa	As authorized; transfers for select purposes authorized by 51 U.S.C. § 20143	Rare
ODNI	• As authorized; Director of National Intelligence (DNI) may reprogram funds within the NIP with the approval of the OMB Director and in consultation with affected agencies • Notification to Congress within 30 days for reprogramming actions >$10M or 5% when funds are transferred in or out of NIP or between appropriation accounts • Notification to Congress of reprogramming actions prior to June 30	As authorized; DNI may transfer funds within NIP with the approval of the OMB Director and in consultation with affected agencies	Detailed funding profiles for NIP and MIP are not publicly available.

Abbreviations

CAPE	Cost Assessment and Program Evaluation
DoD	U.S. Department of Defense
DHS	U.S. Department of Homeland Security
FY	fiscal year
HHS	U.S. Department of Health and Human Services
IPPBE	Intelligence Planning, Programming, Budgeting, and Evaluation
NASA	National Aeronautics and Space Administration
NORAD	North American Aerospace Defense Command
ODNI	Office of the Director of National Intelligence
PPBE	Planning, Programming, Budgeting, and Execution
RDT&E	research, development, test, and evaluation
UK	United Kingdom

References

Canadian Department of National Defence, *Department of National Defence and Canadian Armed Forces, 2022–2023: Departmental Plan*, 2022.

Greenwalt, William, and Dan Patt, *Competing in Time: Ensuring Capability Advantage and Mission Success Through Adaptable Resource Allocation*, Hudson Institute, February 2021.

McGarry, Brendan W., *DOD Planning, Programming, Budgeting, and Execution: Overview and Selected Issues for Congress*, Congressional Research Service, July 11, 2022.

McKernan, Megan, Stephanie Young, Ryan Consaul, Michael Simpson, Sarah W. Denton, Anthony Vassalo, William Shelton, Devon Hill, Raphael S. Cohen, John P. Godges, Heidi Peters, and Lauren Skrabala, *Planning, Programming, Budgeting, and Execution in Comparative Organizations: Vol. 3, Case Studies of Selected Non-DoD Federal Agencies*, RAND Corporation, RR-A2195-3, 2024. As of January 12, 2024: https://www.rand.org/pubs/research_reports/RRA2195-3.html

McKernan, Megan, Stephanie Young, Andrew Dowse, James Black, Devon Hill, Benjamin J. Sacks, Austin Wyatt, Nicolas Jouan, Yuliya Shokh, Jade Yeung, Raphael S. Cohen, John P. Godges, Heidi Peters, and Lauren Skrabala, *Planning, Programming, Budgeting, and Execution in Comparative Organizations: Vol. 2, Case Studies of Selected Allied and Partner Nations*, RAND Corporation, RR-A2195-2, 2024. As of January 12, 2024: https://www.rand.org/pubs/research_reports/RRA2195-2.html

McKernan, Megan, Stephanie Young, Timothy R. Heath, Dara Massicot, Mark Stalczynski, Ivana Ke, Raphael S. Cohen, John P. Godges, Heidi Peters, and Lauren Skrabala, *Planning, Programming, Budgeting, and Execution in Comparative Organizations: Vol. 1, Case Studies of China and Russia*, RAND Corporation, RR-A2195-1, 2024. As of January 12, 2024: https://www.rand.org/pubs/research_reports/RRA2195-1.html

Public Law 117-81, National Defense Authorization Act for Fiscal Year 2022, December 27, 2021.

Section 809 Panel, *Report of the Advisory Panel on Streamlining and Codifying Acquisition Regulations*, Vol. 2 of 3, June 2018.